Text copyright © 2013 Diane Myerson
Illustrations copyright © 2013 Janene Grende

Published in the United States of America
Diane Myerson
Newport Beach, California
www.DianeMyerson.com

Illustrated by
Janene Grende

Book design by
Joel Nelson
Action Printers
Coeur d'Alene, Idaho

ISBN 978-0-980734-4-2
[1. Friendship–Fiction. 2. Animals–Fiction.
3. Adventure–Fiction. 4. Fantasy–Fiction.]

Printed in the United States of America
Action Printers, Coeur d'Alene, Idaho
www.ActionPrinters.net

The Great Carousel Race

By
Diane Myerson

Illustrated By
Janene Grende

This book is a gift for

_____

from

_____

It's the day of the race,
excitement is growing.
Who'll win the grand prize?
There's no way of
knowing.

The animals are ready,
and practice is done.
After hours of waiting,
we'll soon see who's won.

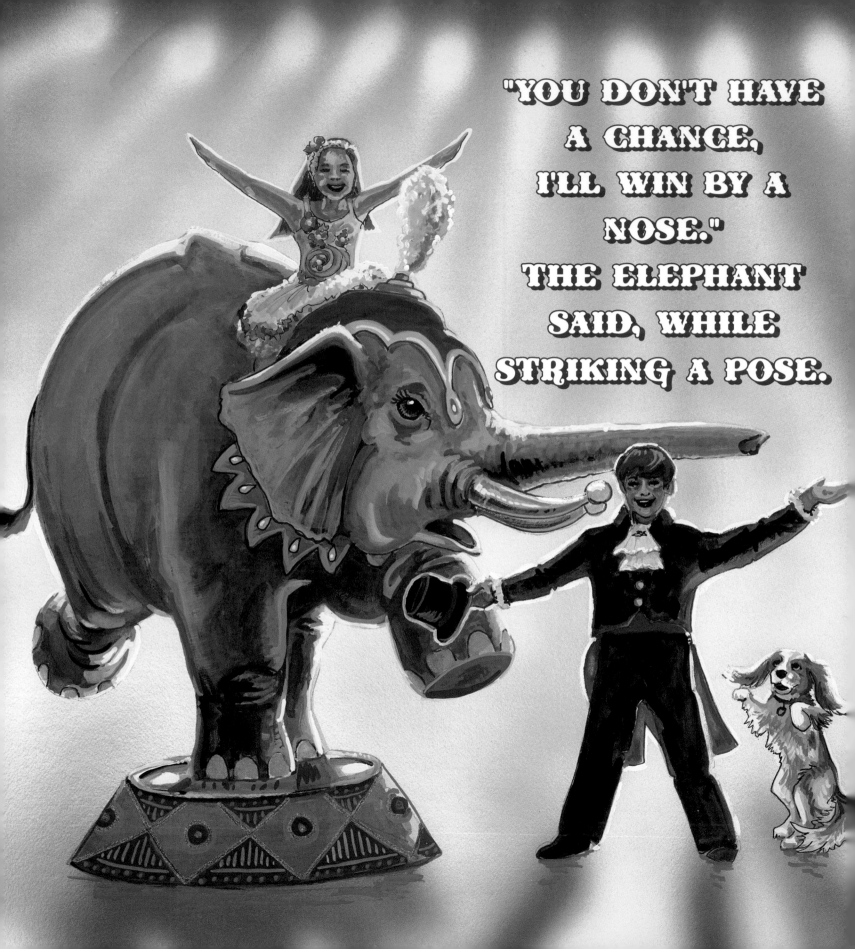

"You can
see I have
feathers,"
the swan said
with a smile.
"I can out fly you,
at least by a mile."

"I've a new saddle," the little pony exclaimed. "Just watch as I pass you, the first place I'll gain."

"Will we ever stop running?"
The lion stifled a yawn.
"I dreamed I was racing
on a beautiful lawn."

THE PANDA BEAR
STRETCHED, WONDERING
WHEN HE'D BE FED.
HE WISHED HE WAS BACK
IN HIS COZY WARM BED.

"Wait just a minute,
I want to run too!"
The giraffe still remembered,
when he lived in a zoo.

The zebra announced,
he had something to tell.
"We all start together,
at the sound of a bell."

The music is playing,
the crowds starting to cheer.
The animals are paw ready,
it is the race of the year.

"I think that I'm winning,"
each said as they passed.
Not knowing that instead,
they really were last.

Around and around
the carousel spun.
The animals galloped,
"Oh this is such fun!"

"Who cares about winning?"
They all said as they passed.
"Just being here together,
make's the fun, last and last!"

Whenever you see,
a carousel spin.
You know all the animals,
are trying to win.

So climb on their backs,
and join in the race.
You might be the winner,
and come in first place!

About The Author

Author with her husband Jim, and Madonna

Diane Myerson has loved carousels her entire life. "There has never been a carousel I didn't have to ride," she says. "The music draws me to the wonderful animals, forever running, forever giving such joy to those who ride on their backs."

'The Great Carousel Race' is Diane's second book about carousels. Her first, 'Robert Wilson's Carousel Clover Ponies', again shares the magic of a carousel. "I've ridden to amazing places where only dreams exist," she explains, "you're never too old to enjoy the ride."

Additional books written and published by Diane Myerson

Robert Wilson's Carousel Clover Ponies

A Little Dog's Christmas Tale

An Invitation To Santa Land

We Believe In Santa Too!

Out of This World Santa

For ordering information please visit:

www.DianeMyerson.com